What's in this book

This book belongs to

_____

第一次露营
Camping for the first time

学习内容 Contents

沟通 Communication

说说日常活动
Talk about your daily routine

生词 New words

★	起床	to get up
★	洗脸	to wash one's face
★	刷牙	to brush one's teeth
★	洗澡	to shower, to bath
★	想	to want to, to think
★	穿	to wear
★	上衣	tops
★	了	(to indicate a change of state or the completion of an action)
	都	both, all
	戴	to wear on top
	条	(measure word for dresses, skirts, pants, etc.)

件　　　　(measure word for tops)

裙子　　dress, skirt

中国儿童的衣服
Clothes worn by Chinese children

句式 Sentence patterns

别的用品都不见了。
The other items are all missing.

你们长大了。
You have grown up.

跨学科学习 Project

制作纸帽子
Fold a paper hat

Get ready

1 Can you name three fun camping activities?

2 Can you take care of yourself when camping?

3 Do you think Hao Hao and his friends can take care of themselves when camping?

dōu
都

第一次一起去露营，同学们都很高兴。

qǐ chuáng
起床

xǐ liǎn
洗脸

shuā yá
刷牙

早上起床后，大家开始洗脸刷牙。

艾文想洗澡，但是他只有毛巾，别的用品都不见了。

爱莎想穿这条裙子，也想穿那件上衣，还想戴帽子。

第一次独立生活，大家都不知道应
该怎么做。

老师说："你们长大了，自己的事应该学习自己做。"

Let's think

1 Recall the activities in the story. Which one did Hao Hao and his friends do? Put a tick or a cross.

2 How well can you do these things? Write the letters.

a 我会做   b 我不太会做   c 我不会做

New words

1 Learn the new words.

起床

刷牙

洗脸、洗澡

想 一条裙子

穿

一件上衣

都戴了帽子

2 Listen to your teacher and point to the correct words above.

听听说说 Listen and say

 1 Listen and circle the correct answers.

2 Look at the pictures. Listen to the story an

1 女孩今天八点做什么？

   a   起床

   b   看书

   c   洗澡

2 女孩穿了什么衣服？

   a   雨衣

   b   长裤

   c   帽子

3 女孩九点做什么？

   a   洗脸

   b   刷牙

   c   洗澡

①

 星期六，我和姐姐不用上学。我们给布朗尼刷牙。

③

 回到家，我们给布朗尼洗澡，它很高兴。

下午，我们去了公园玩，我们一起跑步。

洗了澡，姐姐给布朗尼穿了一件新衣服。小狗真好看！

3 Complete the sentences and role-play with your friend.

a 洗脸 b 洗澡 c 洗手
d 洗衣服 e 刷牙

💬 别玩了，快去___。

💬 别玩了，快去___。

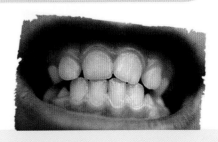

💬 你的牙黄了，快去___。

💬 别玩了，快去___和___。

Task

Write about the things you do during a day. Write the numbers and the time. Talk about them with your friend.

1 洗脸　2 穿衣服　3 做作业　4 起床　5 放学　6 洗澡
7 上床　8 运动　9 玩　10 刷牙　11 上学

活动	星期 _____	
	_____点_____分	星期一，我六点半起床，七点刷牙、洗澡。我早上八点上学，下午三点十五分放学。我四点半做作业，晚上九点半上床。你呢？
	_____点_____分	
	_____点_____分	
	_____点_____分	
	_____点_____分	
	_____点_____分	
	_____点_____分	
	_____点_____分	
	_____点_____分	
	_____点_____分	

Game

Act out the following actions and ask your friend to say the activity in Chinese.

Chant

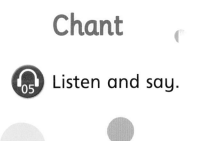

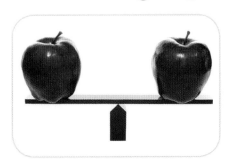

早上六点钟，我们起床、刷牙。
早上六点半，我们洗脸、洗澡。

想一想，今天是晴天还是雨天？
我穿这条长裙，还是那条短裙？
你穿哪件上衣？他穿哪条裤子？

看看天气，穿上衣服，
大家快快乐乐上学去。

生活用语 Daily expressions

都一样。
They are the same.

坏了。

坏了。
It is not working.

写一写 Write

1 Trace and write the characters.

、 、 氵 氵 氵 汒 汒 汫 洗

洗	洗	洗	洗

一 十 土 卡 卡 走 走 起 起 起
、 广 广 庁 床 床

起	床	起	床

2 Write and say.

爱莎说："天气太热了，我要___脸。"

妈妈说："浩浩，八点了，快_____。"

3 Look at the photos and circle the correct words.

大象喜欢（洗澡／洗手）。兔子（rabbit）会（起床／洗脸）。

小猫（穿衣／刷牙）了吗？猴子穿了（帽子／衣服）。小狗穿了

（裙子／裤子）。这些动物真可爱！

拼音输入法 Pinyin input

To type Chinese sentences faster, we can break the sentences into meaningful words instead of individual characters.

1 Type the sentence using two ways. Tick the one which is faster.

早上起床后，大家开始洗脸刷牙。

☐ zao shang qi chuang hou, da jia kai shi xi lian shua ya。

☐ zaoshang qichuang hou, dajia kaishi xilian shuaya。

2 Arrange the words into a meaningful sentence. Write the numbers and type.

xihuan
| 1 喜欢 | 2 洗 | 3 习 ↕ |

☐

ni
| 1 你 | 2 尼 | 3 呢 ↕ |

☐

ma
| 1 马 | 2 妈 | 3 吗 ↕ |

☐

xue
| 1 学 | 2 血 | 3 雪 ↕ |

☐

zhongwen
| 1 中文 | 2 中 | 3 种 ↕ |

☐

?

☐

Cultures

1 Do you think Chinese children wear clothes similar to yours? Read what they say.

我们上学穿校服。

我们在草地上玩，我们穿了球鞋。

新年快乐！我们喜欢在新年穿红色的衣服。

天气冷了，我戴了帽子和围巾。

In ancient China, the emperor and the princesses wore clothes like this. Now we only wear them to take photos.

我学打功夫（kungfu），这是我的功夫衣服。

2 Talk about the clothes the children wear for different occasions.

1 Fold a paper hat.

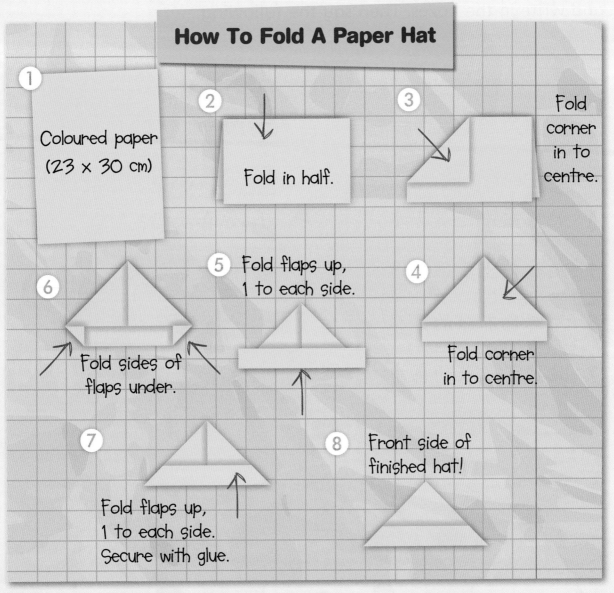

How To Fold A Paper Hat

① Coloured paper (23 x 30 cm)

② Fold in half.

③ Fold corner in to centre.

④ Fold corner in to centre.

⑤ Fold flaps up, 1 to each side.

⑥ Fold sides of flaps under.

⑦ Fold flaps up, 1 to each side. Secure with glue.

⑧ Front side of finished hat!

2 Play with your friends. Wear the hats and talk about them.

我们用纸做帽子，真好玩！

我们都戴了帽子，我最喜欢蓝色的。

我想戴这个帽子去跑步。

温习 Checkpoint

1 Work with your friend. Match the tickets to the pictures and write in the boxes. Then say the following.

1 她想穿	**a** 洗脸。
2 他用两只手	**b** 洗澡？
3 他几点起床？	**c** 刷牙了。
4 她用热水还是冷水	**d** 你喜欢吗？
5 他这件上衣很好看。	**e** 他八点起床。
6 穿绿色衣服的男孩	**f** 和大大的帽子。
7 她戴了长长的围巾	**g** 那条白色的裙子。

走 广

相

20

2 Work with your friend. Colour the stars and the chillies.

Words	说	读	写
起床	☆	☆	☆
洗脸	☆	☆	🌶
刷牙	☆	☆	🌶
洗澡	☆	☆	🌶
想	☆	☆	☆
穿	☆	☆	🌶
上衣	☆	☆	🌶
了	☆	☆	🌶
都	☆	🌶	🌶
戴	☆	🌶	🌶

Words and sentences	说	读	写
条	☆	🌶	🌶
件	☆	🌶	🌶
裙子	☆	🌶	🌶
别的用品都不见了。	☆	🌶	🌶
你们长大了。	☆	🌶	🌶

Talk about daily routine	☆

3 What does your teacher say?

My teacher says...

分享 Sharing

Words I remember

起床	qǐ chuáng	to get up
洗脸	xǐ liǎn	to wash one's face
刷牙	shuā yá	to brush one's teeth
洗澡	xǐ zǎo	to shower, to bath
想	xiǎng	to want to, to think
穿	chuān	to wear
上衣	shàng yī	tops
了	le	(to indicate a change of state or the completion of an action)
都	dōu	both, all
戴	dài	to wear on top
条	tiáo	(measure word for dresses, skirts, pants, etc.)
件	jiàn	(measure word for tops)
裙子	qún zi	dress, skirt

Other words

次	cì	(measure word for frequency)
露营	lù yíng	to go camping
高兴	gāo xìng	happy
只有	zhǐ yǒu	only
后	hòu	afterwards
毛巾	máo jīn	towel
用品	yòng pǐn	articles for use
独立	dú lì	on one's own
应该	yīng gāi	ought to, must
老师	lǎo shī	teacher
长大	zhǎng dà	to grow up
自己	zì jǐ	oneself
事	shì	thing
学习	xué xí	to learn

UNIVERSITY PRESS

Oxford University Press is a department of the University of Oxford.
It furthers the University's objective of excellence in research, scholarship,
and education by publishing worldwide. Oxford is a registered trade mark of
Oxford University Press in the UK and in certain other countries

Published in Hong Kong by
Oxford University Press (China) Limited
39th Floor, One Kowloon, 1 Wang Yuen Street, Kowloon Bay,
Hong Kong

Illustrated by Anne Lee, Emily Chan, KY Chan and Wildman

Photographs for reproduction permitted by Dreamstime.com

China National Publications Import & Export (Group) Corporation is an authorized distributor of
Oxford Elementary Chinese.

Please contact content@cnpiec.com.cn or 86-10-65856782

ISBN: 978-0-19-082256-9

10 9 8 7 6 5 4 3 2